## The American Girls

PENCIL Play

American Girl

Published by Pleasant Company Publications
Copyright © 2004 by American Girl, LLC

Visit our Web site at **americangirl.com.**

Printed in China
04 05 06 07 08 09 10 11 C& C 10 9 8 7 6 5 4 3

Questions or comments?
Call 1-800-845-0005, visit **americangirl.com**, or write to:
American Girl, P.O. Box 620497, Middleton, WI 53562-0497.

The image of the *S.S. Londonia* (p. 44) and the *S.S. Londonia* Morse code card
(p. 30) appear courtesy of becker&mayer! Morse code card design
by J. Max Steinmetz.

Editorial development by Teri Witkowski
Art directed and designed by Will Capellaro and Jane Varda
Produced by Jeannette Bailey, Paula Moon-Bailey,
Mary Cudnohfsky, and Judith Lary
Illustrations by Dan Andreasen, Nick Backes, Bill Farnsworth, Renée Graef,
Susan Moore, Lisa Pfeiffer, John Pugh, Walter Rane, Dahl Taylor,
Jean-Paul Tibbles, and Mike Wimmer

# Contents

# Friends-and-Family Search

The names of the American Girls are hidden in this puzzle along with the names of some of the girls' family members and friends. Can you find them all? The names are shown backward, forward, diagonally, and up and down. Some of the letters will be used for more than one word.

Samantha
Elizabeth
Anna
Clara
Harriet
Nellie
Stirling
Mama
Grandmary
Aunt Inger
Uncle Gard
Francisca
Steps High
Speaking Rain
Miss Manderly

Kit
Jill
Lars
Felicity
Emily
Kaya
Ricky
Kirsten
Lisbeth
Josefina
Sarah
Addy
Molly
Ruthie
Ben

```
S N I A R G N I K A E P S E
O A E Y D R A G E L C N U O
T J M A L K L Y A D P Q A L
N R I A Y I W I T V O N B L
E B S C N A M O S E E P C Y
T C S D P T K E A B S A N S
S G M A M C H N F L E O E T
R N A L R E N A C D A T C E
I I N U L A P D J I N G H P
K L D S T I H D N H I R N S
N R E A D F J Y V A F A T H
A I R I C K Y W X R E N G I
M T L R U T H I E R S D O G
A S Y L L O M Y P I O M L H
M H T E B A Z I L E J A K H
A C S I C N A R F T R R I A
F E L I C I T Y E S K Y T V
J I T E I L L E N C L A R A
L M Y R E G N I T N U A S K
```

1

# Hidden Pictures

Each of these items appears somewhere in this book.
Can you find them all?

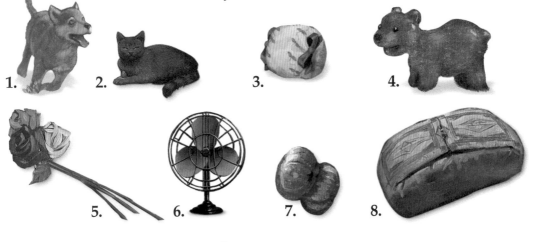

1.  2.  3.  4.

5.  6.  7.  8.

# Match the Past

Can you match all of the people, places, time periods, and phrases to the
right American Girl? Hint: Each American Girl will be used twice.

*a.* Kaya     *c.* Josefina     *e.* Addy     *g.* Kit
*b.* Felicity     *d.* Kirsten     *f.* Samantha     *h.* Molly

__ **1.** George Washington
__ **2.** World War Two
__ **3.** Nimíipuu
__ **4.** Slavery
__ **5.** New Mexico
__ **6.** The Great Depression
__ **7.** Minnesota
__ **8.** New York

__ **9.** Sweden
__ **10.** Cincinnati
__ **11.** American traders
__ **12.** Revolutionary War
__ **13.** Victory gardens
__ **14.** Bitterroot Mountains
__ **15.** Civil War
__ **16.** Suffrage movement

# Amazing Lesson

When Felicity begins her lessons with Miss Manderly, she has plenty to learn. Help her find her way to becoming a gentlewoman. She must pass each lesson in order to finish!

Felicity starts here.

dancing

stitchery

writing

curtsy

serving tea

Felicity finishes as a gentlewoman.

3

# *M*enu Mystery

When Molly and Emily planned an English tea for their birthday party, Molly was surprised at what they'd be eating if they had a *proper* tea. The menu on the left is what Molly wanted to serve. The menu on the right is what Emily suggested. Use the American Girl Code to discover what each girl had in mind.

**Molly's Menu**

**Emily's Menu**

**Bonus question:** Emily explained that she served meat paste sandwiches at tea in England. Molly didn't think her friends would like them at all. What kind of meat was in the sandwiches?

_____

# Horse Match

Kaya could always spot her horse, Steps High, in the herd. Can you? Only two horses are exactly alike. Find them.

# $\mathcal{L}$ost in the Attic

Samantha, Agnes, and Agatha spent the summer exploring the woods, mountains, and waters around Piney Point. One rainy day, the girls stayed inside and explored the attic. Below is a list of some of the things that they found, but parts of these things are still lost. Match the columns to complete the names of the things that the girls found.

*Bonus question:* Samantha was looking for something when she went to the attic. What was it? Use the circled letters to unscramble the answer.

```
H _ O _                        A D S
G l O V E Ⓢ                    A I R
B E O _ _ _                    A N D
H _ O _ B A G S                A T S̶
S h O e S                      B L A
C H _ O _ S                    E T C
A L B O _ _ _                  G L O
S C _ _ O B O O K S            H̶ O E
S K O _ _ H B O O K            L E S
M I O _ _ R                    R A P
C A N D _ _ O T I C K S        R R O
O _ _ _ N K E T S              U M S
```

_ _ _ _ _ _ _ _ _ _ _ _ _

# Grace and the Chicken Race

Help Kit catch Grace, who's chasing the chickens through the yard.
You must pass each chicken to finish.

Start

Finish

# Riddle Game

What game were Poppa and Sam playing in *Changes for Addy*? To find the answer, solve the riddles below, and put the correct letter in each box.

1. I can change *die* into the biggest tip that Addy ever got!
2. Turn *rash* all around and add this near the end to spell the name of Addy's best friend.
3. I am in *nurse* but not *sure*, nor will you find me tucked into a *purse*.
4. I can turn *map* into *camp*, but you'll never find me in the word *lamp*.
5. In *try* I am not, but in *tray* I am caught.
6. Change the last letter in *oven* and move it in front to find what Addy shared with her family.
7. I'm in the center of Addy's *slate* and in *Sam*, *chalk*, and *crate*.

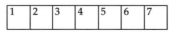

| 1 | 2 | 3 | 4 | 5 | 6 | 7 |
|---|---|---|---|---|---|---|
|   |   |   |   |   |   |   |

# Fall Golds

Josefina's fall was full of many things that were a golden color. Fill in the crossword with some of those things. If you need a hint, check the word list. Then unscramble the circled letters to find something made of dry golden grass that Josefina used every day.

## Across

2. Flowers, herbs, and other _____ were dried for use during the winter.
5. Sombrita kept warm snuggled in _____ on crisp fall nights.
8. Josefina and her sisters harvested lots of _____ from the kitchen garden.
9. Brooms and brushes were made from _____.

## Down

1. Josefina used a stone to grind dried _____ into flour.
3. Josefina loved the bright colors of the _____ that fell from the trees.
4. The days grew shorter in fall, but Josefina had the _____ carved on her memory box.
6. The golden nuts from piñon ____ were harvested in the fall.
7. These fruits were made into bowls and dippers for use in the kitchen.

## Word List

corn
trees
plants
sun
grass
gourds
squash
straw
leaves

__ __ I __ -
B __ __ __ __ H

9

# Find It at the Fair

Circle all the items and activities Addy and her family enjoyed at the church fair. Then write the remaining letters in order from left to right to find something that helped Addy save the day.

cakes
spool puppets
preserves
doughnuts
bread
chicken barbecue
horseshoes
pies
pony rides
ring toss
lemonade
seedlings
popcorn balls
fish fry
games
puppet show
quilts

```
S  A  C  F  C  A  K  E  S
T  S  H  I  P  L  S  W  T
E  I  I  S  O  D  E  O  L
P  E  C  H  P  W  I  H  I
P  S  K  F  C  H  P  S  U
U  E  E  R  O  R  E  T  Q
P  O  N  Y  R  I  D  E  S
L  H  B  G  N  N  A  P  E
O  S  A  A  B  G  N  P  E
O  E  R  M  A  T  O  U  D
P  S  B  E  L  O  M  P  L
S  R  E  S  L  S  E  I  I
S  O  C  T  S  S  L  L  N
E  H  U  D  A  E  R  B  G
P  R  E  S  E  R  V  E  S
S  T  U  N  H  G  U  O  D
```

_ _____ _____

# General Store Scramble

Unscramble the words on
Kirsten's shopping list, then
find each item in the store.

AFGL

NRIO

IRORRM

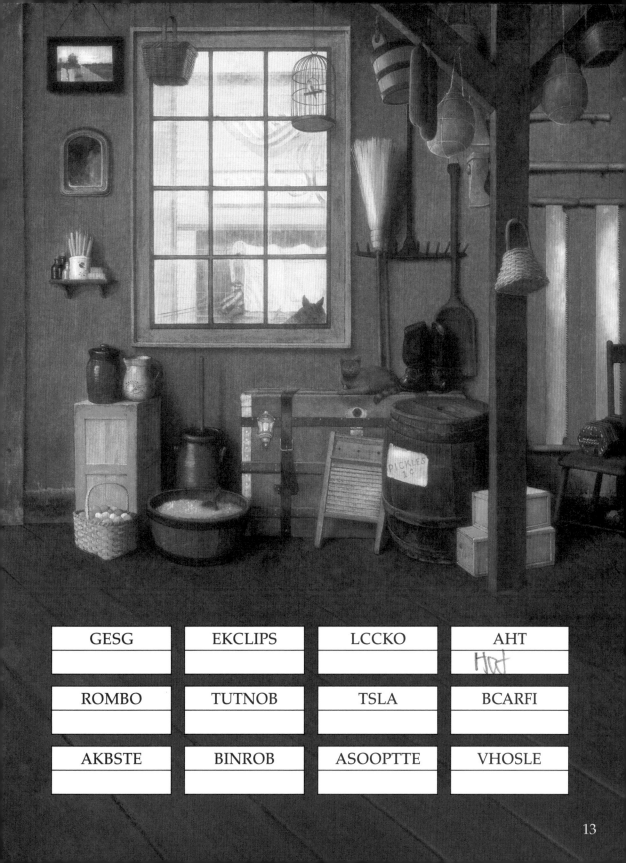

| GESG | EKCLIPS | LCCKO | AHT |
|------|---------|-------|-----|
|  |  |  | Hat |

| ROMBO | TUTNOB | TSLA | BCARFI |
|-------|--------|------|--------|
|  |  |  |  |

| AKBSTE | BINROB | ASOOPTTE | VHOSLE |
|--------|--------|----------|--------|
|  |  |  |  |

Kaya

Felicity

Josefina

Kirsten

Addy

Samantha

Kit

Molly

H _ _ _ _ _ _ _

A T _ _ _ _ _ _

E _ _ _ _

C _ _ _ _

R B E A _ _ _ _

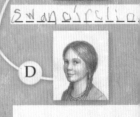

Evangelina

D _ _ _ _ _ _ _ _ _

_ _ _ _ _

# Friends at the End

Help the American Girls find their friends. As you travel each path, write down the letters that you cross to reveal the name of the friend at the end!

14

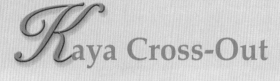

# Kaya Cross-Out

The name "Kaya" is a shortened version of the Nez Perce word *Kaya'aton'my'*. What does this name mean? Follow the instructions below, then read the answer.

1. Cross out 4 fruits.
2. Cross out 3 seasons.
3. Cross out 2 shapes.
4. Cross out 3 animals.
5. Cross out 4 ways to move.

| | | | | |
|---|---|---|---|---|
| SHE | ~~APPLE~~ | ~~SKIP~~ | ~~WINTER~~ | ~~ORANGE~~ |
| ~~SUMMER~~ | WHO | ~~CIRCLE~~ | ~~WALK~~ | ARRANGES |
| ~~RACCOON~~ | ~~JUMP~~ | SQUIRREL | BANANA | ~~RUN~~ |
| ~~SQUARE~~ | ~~HORSE~~ | ~~PEAR~~ | SPRING | ROCKS |

# Top Secret Code

Molly and her friends wrote messages in code when they were
Top Secret Agents. Make a decoder to solve the secrets in
these sentences. You'll need the following supplies:
wide-lined notebook paper, tape, scissors, a pencil, and a paper clip.

**1** Cut 2 half-inch-
wide strips of
wide-lined paper.
Using the lines as
dividers, write the
letters A to Z on one
strip and the num-
bers 1 to 26 on the
other.

**2** Tape the ends
of each strip
together into a
ring and fasten the
2 rings together
with a paper clip.

**3** The paper clip
shows the key to
your code. When the
clip shows A=7,
MOLLY is spelled
19-21-18-18-5.
Change the key, and
you can change the
code!

## The key is A+12
**1.** To win the color war, Molly had to 4-8-20-24 6-25-15-16-3-8-12-5-16-3.

_ _ _ _ / _ _ _ _ _ _ _ _ _

**2.** Linda and Susan gave Molly their 24-26-7-20-16 money so Molly could buy a 1-16-3-24-12-25-16-25-5 8-12-7-16 kit.

_ _ _ _ _ / _ _ _ _ _ _ _ _ / _ _ _ _

**3.** Mrs. McIntire added 4-6-18-12-3, 13-6-5-5-16-3, and 14-20-25-25-12-24-26-25 to the 5-6-3-25-20-1-4 so Molly could finish them.

_ _ _ _ _ / _ _ _ _ _ _ / _ _ _ _ _ _ _ _ / _ _ _ _ _ _

## Change the key to M+3
**4.** Molly and her friends collected 18-5-10-10-2-21-10-5-6-9 for the 2-21-4-20 17 24-17-4-20 contest.

_ _ _ _ _ _ _ _ _ / _ _ _ _ / _ / _ _ _ _

**5.** When Emily came to stay with the McIntires, she brought a 9-19-8-17-6-18-5-5-1 full of 6-25-19-10-11-8-21-9 of the English 6-8-25-4-19-21-9-9-21-9.

_ _ _ _ _ _ _ _ / _ _ _ _ _ _ _ _ / _ _ _ _ _ _ _ _ _

**6.** Molly and Jill's secret mission was to 24-25-20-21 the 18-5-14 from 20-17-20 until 19-24-8-25-9-10-3-17-9.

_ _ _ _ / _ _ _ / _ _ _ /_ _ _ _ _ _ _ _

## Now use O+22 as the key
**7.** When 25-16-10-18-6 ruined their 15-8-19-19-22-4-12-12-21 1-25-12-8-1-26, Molly, Susan, and Linda got even by 11-2-20-23-16-21-14 his 2-21-11-12-25-4-12-8-25 out the window.

_ _ _ _ _ / _ _ _ _ _ _ _ _ / _ _ _ _ _ _ / _ _ _ _ _ _ _ / _ _ _ _ _ _ _ _

**8.** Molly was chosen to be 20-16-26-26 3-16-10-1-22-25-6 in the 15-2-25-25-8-6 for the 2-26-8 show.

_ _ _ _ / _ _ _ _ _ _ _ / _ _ _ _ _ _ / _ _ _

**9.** The 26-1-22-25-8-14-12 room above the 14-8-25-8-14-12 was Molly, Linda, and Susan's private 10-19-2-9-15-22-2-26-12.

_ _ _ _ _ _ _ / _ _ _ _ _ _ / _ _ _ _ _ _ _ _

# Kaya's Crossword

Kaya was growing up in 1764, before America was a country. She loved her family, her horse, and games of all kinds. Complete the puzzle to discover more about Kaya and her world. If you get stuck, check the word list.

**Word List**
berries
grandmother
tepees
drums
fish
native
dog
brothers
horse
blind
animals
mountain
race
nickname
captured

## Down:

**1.** Kaya was a _____ American who would today be known as a Nez Perce Indian.

**2.** Many Nez Perce people were named for _____, like Brown Deer, Sparrow, and Swan Circling.

**5.** Kaya befriended a lone _____ that was about to have puppies.

**6.** The women in Kaya's family built the _____ that everyone slept in.

**7.** Kaya had two sisters and two _____.

**8.** After she escaped, Kaya had to climb a steep and rocky _____ to get back home.

**9.** Her mother's mother, or her _____, was Kaya's teacher.

## Across:

**3.** She knew her horse could run fast, so Kaya agreed to a _____.

**4.** Speaking Rain could not see. She was _____.

**10.** Kaya enjoyed the sweet _____ she picked off bushes.

**11.** In the evenings, Kaya's people danced and sang to the beat of the _____.

**12.** The other children called Kaya Magpie, which was a _____ she hated.

**13.** Kaya and her sister were _____ by enemy raiders and taken from their camp.

**14.** The beautiful Appaloosa _____ Kaya rode was named Steps High.

**15.** Kaya's people went to the river to _____ for food.

# aily Maze

After her evening meal each day, Josefina sat in front of the fire and practiced *colcha*. Help Josefina thread her way through the maze, picking up the letters along the way to spell out what colcha is.

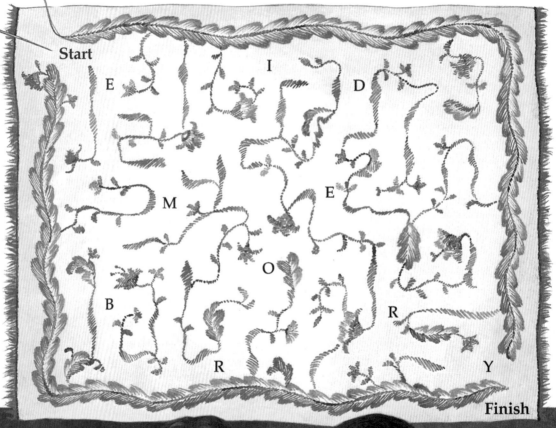

# Toy Story Memory

Study the toys in the store window for several minutes, then turn the page to see how much you remember about the picture.

# $\mathcal{T}$oy Story Memory (continued)

**Don't read this until you have read page 21!**
Circle the toys that were in the window. *No peeking!*

| | | | | |
|---|---|---|---|---|
| teddy bear | ball | crayons | clown | baby doll |
| yo-yo | jacks | seal | tea set | nutcracker doll |
| toy soldier | elephant | rooster | boat | ballerina doll |
| hula hoop | giraffe block | | | |

## $\mathcal{N}$ame the Game

Kit and Stirling were both fans of this game. To find out what it is, cross out all the letters that appear four times. Then write the remaining letters in the spaces below.

T R I O B T
H M P G A T
S U G P H E
R P J M I B
M A J R H O
L T H U G O
P U I L O J
M G J R I U

_ _ _ _ _ _ _

# 𝒫atchwork Puzzle

Kirsten, Anna, Lisbeth, and Mary are stitching four different
quilt patterns with four different fabrics in four different colors.
Using the clues below, can you fill in the grid to show who is
making which pattern out of what fabric and color?

|  | ANNA | LISBETH | KIRSTEN | MARY |
|---|---|---|---|---|
| PATTERN |  |  |  |  |
| COLOR |  |  |  |  |
| FABRIC |  |  |  |  |

**1.** Anna is making a
wreath pattern.
**2.** The flower pattern
is made in blue.
**3.** The silk fabric is used
for a heart.

**4.** The muslin fabric is
not used for the flower
pattern.
**5.** The starburst pattern
is not made in brown.
**6.** The linen fabric is blue.

**7.** Lisbeth's fabric is white.
**8.** The wreath is made of
calico.
**9.** Mary's fabric is red.
**10.** Lisbeth is not making
a heart.

# Color a Message

Felicity gave her sampler to Elizabeth as a secret message. What were the words she had stitched? Find out by coloring all the M's, C's, and J's in the puzzle below.

```
M F C C J A I T C J H M
F J U M L C M F R C I J
E C M N D J C S F M O R
M E J V E C M R J B M E
```

Faithful Friends Forever Be

# Writer's Crossword

Kit's writing a newspaper article, but the words below aren't quite right. Find another word that means the same thing to complete the puzzle. If you need a hint, check the thesaurus.

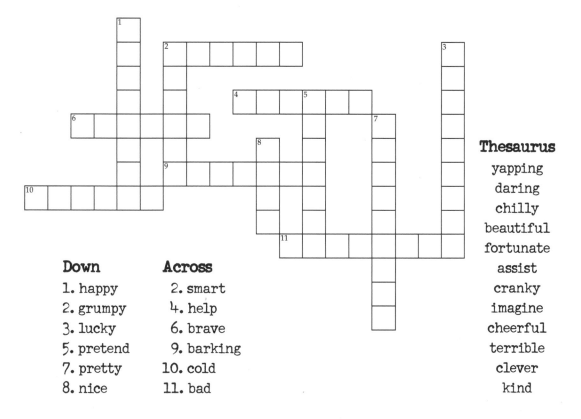

**Thesaurus**

yapping
daring
chilly
beautiful
fortunate
assist
cranky
imagine
cheerful
terrible
clever
kind

**Down**
1. happy
2. grumpy
3. lucky
5. pretend
7. pretty
8. nice

**Across**
2. smart
4. help
6. brave
9. barking
10. cold
11. bad

Classroom Quiz

Study Molly's classroom for several minutes,
then turn the page to test your memory.

# Classroom Quiz (continued)

***Don't read this until you have read page 27!***
How much do you remember about Molly's classroom?
Answer these questions to find out. No peeking!

**1.** What month was on the calendar?
**2.** What was the last task on the list of "things to do today" on the chalkboard?
**3.** What was the color of the building outside the window?
**4.** What was in the cup next to the vase of flowers on the desk?
**5.** What time did the clock read?
**6.** How many American flags were there in the scene?
**7.** True or false: there was a tank of fish in the classroom.
**8.** What color were the flowers on the windowsill?

# Friends Forever

The American Girls all knew what it took to be true friends. Can you find their seven keys to lasting friendship?

loyalty
heart
sharing
trust
faith
love
caring

```
        C Y I J           B C X P
      O O S E L Z     W F J C Q L
      T S E R Y U T S U R T N O
      Q N H C G A S F C M D J G
      G V K A L O Y A L T Y C R
      S A D Y R B R I A X T M D
      C M G H T I O T R F R D
      X D O N Z N H V L A P
        J I G B C R G O K E
        U K P F D V N X F
          T R A E H O M
          I F V C I
          Z M Y
          H
```

# Spanish Match

Josefina grew up speaking Spanish in New Mexico. Spanish people were in North America long before the Pilgrims, and they gave lots of places Spanish names. See if you can match each Spanish place name on the left with its English meaning on the right.

**1.** Arizona     The Pass
**2.** Rio Grande     Flowery
**3.** Santa Fe     Holy Faith
**4.** Los Angeles     Mountain
**5.** El Paso     Colored Red
**6.** Montana     Arid Zone
**7.** Colorado     The Angels
**8.** Florida     Big River

# Morse Code Messages

Samantha joined Grandmary and the Admiral for a grand vacation aboard the *S.S. Londonia*. Use the Morse code alphabet to discover what she did on her journey.

**1.** Grandmary let Samantha stay up until
--M•• I--••D-•_••_--_•••_-_
for the ship's •-••_•-_••-_-•_-•-_•••_.

**2.** Samantha and Grandmary had -_•_•-_in the
--_-•-•_•_•-_-•_/--•_•-_•-•_
-••_•_-•_room, which was full of
•--•_•-••_•-_-•_-_•••_and
-•••_••_•-•_-••_•••_.

**3.** On deck, Samantha played -_••-_--•_/
---_•-•_/•-_•-_••-_and won the
•_--•_--•_/•-_-•_-••_/
•••_•-•-_-_---_-_-•_race.

S.S. LONDONIA
MORSE CODE

| | | | |
|---|---|---|---|
| A | •- | N | -• |
| B | -••• | O | --- |
| C | -•-• | P | •--• |
| D | -•• | Q | --•- |
| E | • | R | •-• |
| F | ••-• | S | ••• |
| G | --• | T | - |
| H | •••• | U | ••- |
| I | •• | V | •••- |
| J | •--- | W | •-- |
| K | -•- | X | -••- |
| L | •-•• | Y | -•-- |
| M | -- | Z | --•• |

**4.** Samantha wanted to visit the

-•-•__•-__•-•__-••__/•-•__- - -__- - -__--__ ,

but •-••__•-__-••__••__•__•••__were not

•-__•-••__•-••__- - -__•--__•__-••__.

**5.** The -•-•__•-__•-•-__-__•-__••__-•__ asked Samantha,

Grandmary, and the Admiral to •- - -__- - -__••__-•__ him for

-••__••__-•__-•__•__•-•__ at the captain's -__•-__-•••__

•-••__ •__ , which was quite an •••__- - -__-•__- - -__•-•__!

**6.** Grandmary got •••__•__•-__•••__••__-•-•__-•-__ and

had to take two big •••__•- - •__- - -__- - -__-•__•-•__••-__

•-••__•••__ of --__•__-••__••__-•-•__••__-•__•__.

**7.** Samantha couldn't •- - -__•-__••__ -__ to attend the captain's

--•__•-__•-••__•-__/-•••__•-__•-••__•-••__ in the

--•__•-•__•-__-•__-••__/-•••__•-__•-••__•-••__

•-•__- - -__- - -__--__.

**8.** Samantha practiced her dots and dashes so she could write messages in code. Now it's your turn! Try writing the message Samantha sent to Agnes and Agatha using Morse code. Use slashes to separate the words.

*Wish you were here.*
*I've been exploring. Love, Sam.*

**9.** Samantha also sent a message to Uncle Gard, Aunt Cornelia, Nellie, Bridget, and Jenny: *I miss you all.*

# Treasures from the Trunk

Kirsten was eager to unpack the things her family had brought all the way from Sweden. Find each of the items she found in the trunk. The words are shown backward, forward, diagonally, and up and down. Some of the letters will be used for more than one word.

```
L F Y B J M G Y R B C P E J I
T A O C I T T E P A L I L W M
M S S M C V L O N P Y L B V D
S D G M S T A D O G J L I D Z
Q H I N S T L E L R H O B I S
D V A I I E O O H E C W K L N
L U H W S K L O M T S C O T N
R W G T L B C D B A M O O J Q
P N I B T S L O V E T V Q B Z
Q C O T R H K A T W S E S O S
K W L A N T E R N S B R D P E
L P L A T E T D V K S B O D A
W V K W S I T L N N E O L V J
T E N N O B L P Z P N T L O T
R K U M P L E M E S H L N G Y
```

doll
boots
petticoat
sweater
lantern
tools
bonnet
whistle
kettle
blanket

Bible
pillowcover
plate
shawl
candlestick
bowl
spoons
stockings

# $\mathcal{S}$tates in a Circle

Kaya's people traveled with the seasons to gather food and to hunt and fish. They lived in the mountains, prairies, and canyons of what today are three separate states. Solve the puzzles below to find out which states they are.

B
D    O
H              I
T    Start at "B," counting     W
it as your first letter.
Move clockwise, and        F
R    write down every fourth
letter on the lines below.      N
K    _ _ _ _ _ _ -
N
S    _ _ _
G            A
E    L

K
P        V
G
D
R    W        O        B
E    Start at "K," counting        F              K
it as your first letter.
Move clockwise, and write    O    W    Start at "O," counting    A
A    down every fifth letter on        X    it as your first letter.
the lines below.    B    D    Move clockwise, and write    S
N        _ _ _ _ _ _ J        L    down every seventh letter
V        on the lines below.    M
C    R    M    O        E    _ _ _ _ _    I
H    R
T    C

33

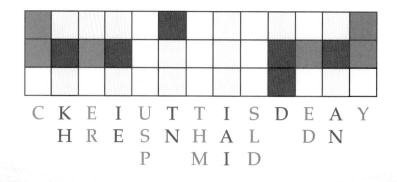

# Christmas Surprise

Put the letters in each column into the boxes above them.
You must decide which letter goes into which box in each
column. A letter can be used only once. Leave the red and green
boxes empty. When all the letters are placed correctly, you'll find
out what Molly's dad wrote on a special Christmas package.

```
C   K   E   I   U   T   T   I   S   D   E   A   Y
    H   R   E   S   N   H   A   L       D   N
        P       M   I   D
```

# Riddle Cross-Out

Addy's brother Sam loved to ask Addy riddles. Try solving this one: **What can turn without moving?** Follow the instructions below, then read the answer.

1. Cross out 3 ways to get to school.
2. Cross out 3 sports that use balls.
3. Cross out 4 kinds of candy.
4. Cross out 2 ways to laugh.
5. Cross out 3 things that ring.

| | | | | |
|---|---|---|---|---|
| TELEPHONE | GUMDROPS | BOWLING | MILK | BIKE |
| WHEN | CHUCKLE | BELL | TAFFY | IT |
| TENNIS | BUS | TURNS | SOCCER | GIGGLE |
| WALK | SOUR | LICORICE | ALARM | CHOCOLATE |

# Boarding House Hunt

Kit's family took in boarders to earn enough money to keep their house during the Depression. They had to make room for more people—and more things. See what you can find in this picture.

1. How many places are there to sleep? 6
2. Where is the telephone? The Kitchen
3. Find the pink and white blanket. The living room
4. Can you spot the bowl of fruit? The kitchen
5. Find the radio.
6. There are six towels in this picture. Can you find them all?
7. Find the baseball glove.
8. How many alarm clocks can you find?
9. Can you spot two pairs of eyeglasses?
10. There are four mirrors in three different rooms. Find them all.
11. Find a broom.
12. Where's the iron?
13. Find the purple shirt.
14. Where's the wastebasket?
15. There are three green chairs in the kitchen. Find the fourth somewhere else in the house.

# 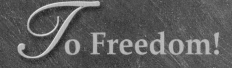o Freedom!

Felicity set Penny free because Jiggy Nye mistreated her. Help Penny find her way to the woods by starting at the F in the upper left corner. Move up and down or across, but not diagonally, to spell the word "Freedom" over and over until you reach the woods. You must use every letter.

*Penny* →
```
F R E O M E E
O D E D F R D
M E E E F M O
F R D E R E E
F M O R F O D
R E D O M M F
D E E E E E R
O M F R D O M  → Woods
```

# Sewing Shop Scramble

After Addy and her mother escaped from slavery, Momma got a job as a seamstress in Mrs. Ford's dress shop. Addy helped by making deliveries after school. She worked hard and waited for the day her father, brother, and sister would join them in Philadelphia. Unscramble the letters that spell the items in Mrs. Ford's shop. If you get stuck, check the word list. Then unscramble the letters that appear in the circles to reveal Momma's message to Addy.

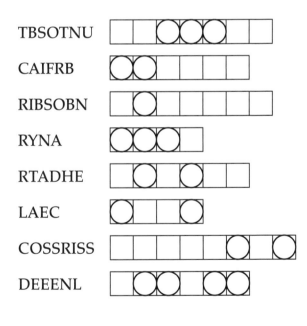

TBSOTNU

CAIFRB

RIBSOBN

RYNA

RTADHE

LAEC

COSSRISS

DEEENL

**Word List**
thread
yarn
scissors
ribbons
lace
fabric
buttons
needle

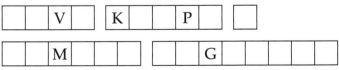

| | V | | K | | P | | |

| | M | | | | | G | | | | |

# Secrets Solved

Do you know the secrets of the American Girls? Test your sleuthing skills with this puzzle. If you need a hint, check the word list.

## Across:

2. Felicity sneaked out of her house for secret rides with a horse named after a copper coin.

5. Felicity kept this boy's hiding place a secret, because he was her friend.

8. Samantha taught Nellie lessons in a secret place at the top of Grandmary's house.

10. Josefina and Francisca secretly went to Santa Fe in the middle of the night to get this stringed instrument for Papá.

12. Molly and Jill kept Dad's box a secret by hiding it under something that's usually on a bed.

13. Stirling secretly used the machine on Kit's desk to write a letter.

17. Felicity discovered the governor's secret plan to steal a kind of powder.

18. Kirsten secretly tried to get this sweet treat from a bee tree in the forest.

19. Addy saved her money for a warm, woolly Christmas gift for Momma to wear

## Down:

1. This secret native American friend taught Kirsten to whistle like a meadowlark.

3. Kaya kept the reason she got this kind of name a secret from her friend, Swan Circling.

4. Addy overheard her parents' secret plan to run away, or _____.

6. Josefina's sister Clara secretly hid a doll in a type of box.

7. Kirsten needed something she wore to bed for her secret St. Lucia celebration.

9. Samantha secretly helped Nellie and her sisters run away from this gloomy place.

11. Kit wanted a Robin Hood party to celebrate her special day.

14. Aunt Millie didn't make it a secret that Kit's family was trying to save this.

15. Josefina secretly hoped Papá would propose to Tía Dolores so they would _____.

16. Molly, Linda, and Susan called themselves the Top Secret kind of

**Word List**

scarf
gunpowder
blanket
Ben
nightgown
money
typewriter

feed
Coldrock House
penny
nickname
escape
honey
agents

Singing Bird
attic
violin
trunk
marry
birthday

# Fandango Fun

Josefina's grandfather was a trader who led a caravan of goods from Mexico City every year. In the first puzzle, find some of the items he would have brought home with him. The words can appear forward, backward, up, down, or diagonally.

| | | | |
|---|---|---|---|
| china | lace | spices |
| dishes | silver | tools |
| jewelry | silk | |

```
J D I S H E S
T E T O C E P
K L W O E B I
L R A E O T C
I E C A L L E
S I L V E R S
E C H I N A Y
```

Now find some of the makings for a *fandango*, or party, in the second puzzle.

cookies    flowers    piano
dancing    music    stories
food    rebozo    lemonade
fiddle    pianist

Write down the unused letters in order from left to right, starting with the first puzzle, to see why Josefina's village had a fandango each time a caravan arrived.

```
F T S I N A I P
D L T S A F P E
A E O M U S I C
N M R W R R A E
C O I F E E N L
I N E O B R O D
N A S O O T S D
G D U D Z R N I
S E I K O O C F
```

\_\_ _____

A _____ _____

43

# Ship-Speak Scramble

During her trip on the *S.S. Londonia*, Samantha learned "ship speak" for many of the things and places on an ocean liner. The underlined words are hidden in the puzzle below. They may be shown backward, forward, diagonally, or up and down. Some of the letters will be used for more than one word.

1. Samantha's room was called a <u>cabin</u>.
2. On a ship, windows are called <u>portholes</u>.
3. The meals are prepared in the ship's enormous <u>galley</u>.
4. When Samantha took a walk around the deck, she was <u>above deck</u>.
5. <u>Port</u> is the left side of the ship.
6. Samantha met Annie on the <u>steerage</u> deck, which is for third-class passengers.
7. A toilet is called a <u>head</u>.
8. <u>Starboard</u> is the right side of the ship.
9. The captain directs the course of the ship from the <u>bridge</u>.
10. Anyone on a ship is <u>aboard</u> a ship.
11. A <u>squall</u> is a sudden, violent wind often accompanied by rain.
12. Samantha would <u>stow</u> her scrapbook and camera so they didn't fall on the floor when the seas got rough.
13. The crew kept watch from a platform called a <u>crow's nest</u> high atop the ship's mast.
14. Samantha walked down a ramp called a <u>gangplank</u> to leave the ship.

```
T R O P L S U C M E H D Y B A W I N Y
K N A L P G N A G R G R B O R N O E C
S Q U A L L K B G B D A G X A I L T H
W V L U F C R I G Y Z O R D W L D E S
X R E Z I E K N B S T B S E A S A G G
S T A R B O A R D A J A K G E D J X E
J C R O W S N E S T S E L O H T R O P
K C E D E V O B A R M D B N G A S G J
```

# Animal Affections

Kaya's people respected and loved animals, and many Nez Perces were named for them. Use the American Girl code to discover the names of some of Kaya's family and friends.

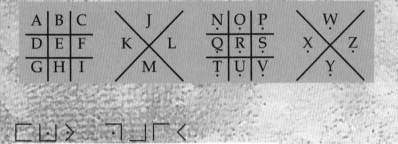

| A | B | C | | J | | N | O | P | | W | |
|---|---|---|---|---|---|---|---|---|---|---|---|
| D | E | F | K | | L | Q | R | S | X | | Z |
| G | H | I | | M | | T | U | V | | Y | |

# *G*ifts of Giving

The American Girls found lots of ways to help their families, friends, and neighbors. Solve the puzzle to discover how they made a difference by being kind, doing their best, and keeping hope alive. If you need a hint, check the word list.

**Across**

2. When Nellie was in the orphanage, Samantha gave her a pair of _____ to stay warm.
4. Felicity borrowed a pair of Ben's _____ to wear when she went to see Penny.
5. Kit's class donated food to a soup _____ on Thanksgiving.
7. In Addy's time, aid societies were formed to help escaped _____.
12. Josefina loved to go to trading _____, where Mexicans, Americans, Indians, and settlers brought their goods.
13. In southern _____ like Virginia, where Felicity lived, people prided themselves on their hospitality.
14. The Larsons and their neighbors shared, traded, and ____ each other with everything.
15. A _____ raising was a community event for the Larsons.
16. Samantha's ____ was a suffragist, someone who worked for women's right to vote.

## Word List

| | |
|---|---|
| gloves | electric |
| princess | name |
| kitchen | basket |
| aunt | garden |
| fairs | scrap |
| skills | barn |
| colonies | helped |
| slaves | breeches |
| victory | |

## Down

1. Kit earned enough money to pay the _____ bill by working for her uncle.

3. Kit wrote a story for her best friend called "The Story of _____ Ruthie."

6. Swan Circling wanted Kaya to have her _____.

7. Molly and her friends held _____drives, variety shows, and box socials to help the war effort.

8. The McIntires and Mrs. Gilford planted a _____ garden.

9. Tía Dolores shared her many ____ with Josefina and her sisters.

10. Before she married, Kaya's sister gave Cut Cheek's parents a _____ of dried roots as a gift.

11. The Walkers planted a vegetable _____to raise money to find Esther, Uncle Solomon, and Auntie Lula.

# Create a Code

Kit met a young hobo named Will, who rode the rails looking for work. Will taught Kit some of the hobo code, which was a language of symbols that were drawn on fences, buildings, or the sidewalk. Hobos used these symbols to let each other know what to expect in a new place.

Below are some of the symbols Kit learned. Use the spaces on the bottom of the fence to create your own secret code to use with your friends.

Free tele-phone

You can sleep in this barn.

Work avail-able

Kind lady

I've got big news to share.

Sleep-over tonight.

I need home-work help.

Meet me at lunch.

Keep
quiet.

These
people
will help
if you're
sick.

Doctor
will treat
without
charge.

Bad
dog
here

Call me.

I'm in a
bad
mood.

Come
over
after
school.

You're
invited
to a
birthday
party.

49

# $\int$ tories to Celebrate

The American Girls had lots of reasons to celebrate. With hard work and hope, their dreams came true. Discover the moments that made them happiest by unscrambling the boxes after each clue.

**1.** She discovers something she once set free.

| | |
|---|---|
| ER H | FIN |
| DS H | CITY |
| ORSE | FELI |
| NY | PEN |

_____ _____ _____
_____ _____

**2.** She hears wedding bells for her papá.

| | | |
|---|---|---|
| TIA | S FA | RIES |
| MAR | THER | FINA |
| DOL | JOSE | ORES |

_____ _____ _____
_____ _____

**4.** She must leave her sister behind when she escapes from enemy raiders.

| IS R | KAYA | WITH |
|------|------|------|
| IN | AKIN | SPE |
| G RA | EUNI | TED |

_____ _____ _____

_____ _____ _____

**3.** She's thrilled to have her dad back in the USA.

| ME F | S HO | |
|------|------|------|
| MOLL | ROM | ATHE |
| R RE | TURN | WAR |
| THE | YS F | |

_____ _____ _____

_____ _____

_____

**5.** She makes a difference by writing her opinion.

| NEWS | TER | KIT'S |
|------|-----|-------|
| IS P | LET | IN |
| PAPE | SHED | UBLI |
| R | THE | |

_____ _____ _____

_____ _____ _____

**6.** She's an orphan who gets sisters of her own.

| ELLI | D HE | R SI |
|------|------|------|
| STER | ADOP | CLE |
| NTHA | SAMA | E AN |
| TS N | S UN | S |

_____ _____ _____

_____ _____ _____

**7.** She and her mother are separated from the rest of their family when they escape from slavery in North Carolina.

| MILY | N IN | S FA |
|------|------|------|
| ADDY | TOGE | AGAI |
| IS | ADEL | PHIL |
| | PHIA | THER |

\_\_\_\_\_  \_\_\_\_\_  \_\_\_\_\_

\_\_\_\_\_  \_\_\_\_\_  \_\_\_\_\_

\_\_\_\_\_

**8.** She dreamed of a home in America.

| THE | HOUSE |
|-----|-------|
| GETS | TENS |
| FAM | IR V |
| ERY | OWN |
| ILY | KIRS |

\_\_\_\_\_  \_\_\_\_\_  \_\_\_\_\_

\_\_\_\_\_  \_\_\_\_\_  \_\_\_\_\_

\_\_\_\_\_

**9.** Something you can do to make your secret wishes come true.

| OUR | DREA |
|-----|------|
| TO Y | HOLD |
| MS | ON |

\_\_\_\_\_  \_\_\_\_\_

\_\_\_\_\_  \_\_\_\_\_

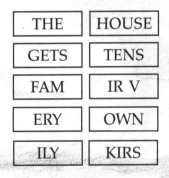

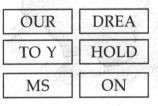

Answers

## Friends-and-Family Search, page 1

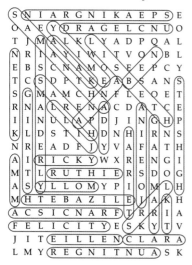

## Hidden Pictures, page 2

1. page 45
2. page 13
3. page 24
4. page 21
5. page 30
6. page 26
7. page 7
8. page 33

## Match the Past, page 2

1. b
2. h
3. a
4. e
5. c
6. g
7. d
8. f
9. d
10. g
11. c
12. b
13. h
14. a
15. e
16. f

## Amazing Lesson, page 3

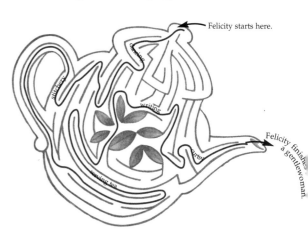

Felicity starts here.

Felicity finishes a gentlewoman.

54

## Menu Mystery, page 4

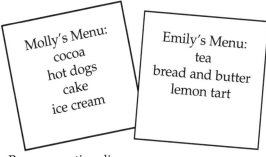

Molly's Menu:
cocoa
hot dogs
cake
ice cream

Emily's Menu:
tea
bread and butter
lemon tart

Bonus question: liver

## Grace and the Chicken Race, page 7

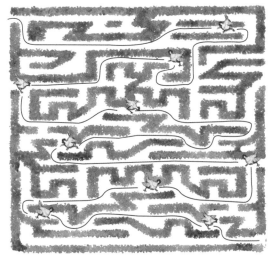

## Horse Match, page 5

## Riddle Game, page 8

mancala

## Fall Golds, page 9

hairbrush

## Find It at the Fair, page 10

a slide whistle

## Lost in the Attic, page 6

hats          shoes          sketchbook
gloves        chairs         mirror
beads         albums         candlesticks
handbags      scrapbooks     blankets

Bonus question: paintbrushes

## General Store Scramble, page 12

Match these numbers to image above.

| | |
|---|---|
| 1. flag | 9. ribbon |
| 2. iron | 10. clock |
| 3. mirror | 11. salt |
| 4. eggs | 12. potatoes |
| 5. broom | 13. hat |
| 6. basket | 14. fabric |
| 7. pickles | 15. shovel |
| 8. button | |

## Top Secret Code, page 16

1. swim underwater
2. movie, permanent wave
3. sugar, butter, cinnamon, turnips
4. bottletops, lend a hand
5. scrapbook, pictures, princesses
6. hide, box, Dad, Christmas
7. Ricky, Halloween treats, dumping, underwear
8. Miss Victory, hurray, USA
9. storage, garage, clubhouse

## Friends at the End, page 14

Kaya and Swan Circling
Felicity and Elizabeth
Josefina and Mariana
Kirsten and Singing Bird
Addy and Sarah
Samantha and Nellie
Kit and Ruthie
Molly and Linda

## Kaya Cross-Out, page 15

she who arranges rocks

## Kaya's Crossword, page 18

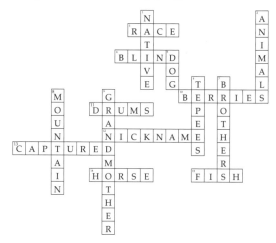

## Daily Maze, page 20

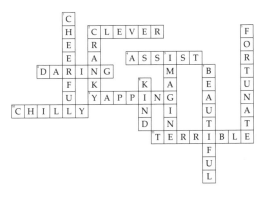

## Toy Story Memory, page 22

teddy bear

toy soldier

ball

giraffe block

seal

rooster

clown

boat

nutcracker doll

ballerina doll

## Name the Game, page 22

baseball

## Patchwork Puzzle, page 23

|         | ANNA   | LISBETH  | KIRSTEN | MARY  |
|---------|--------|----------|---------|-------|
| PATTERN | wreath | starburst| flower  | heart |
| COLOR   | brown  | white    | blue    | red   |
| FABRIC  | calico | muslin   | linen   | silk  |

## Color a Message, page 24

Faithful friends forever be.

## Writer's Crossword, page 25

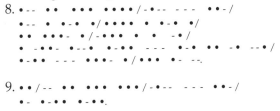

## Classroom Quiz, page 28

1. September
2. clean desks
3. yellow
4. pencils
5. 8:54
6. two
7. False. There was a turtle in the tank.
8. red

## Friends Forever, page 28

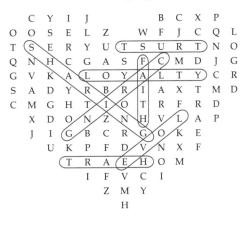

## Spanish Match, page 29

1. Arid Zone
2. Big River
3. Holy Faith
4. The Angels
5. The Pass
6. Mountain
7. Colored Red
8. Flowery

## Morse Code Messages, page 30

1. midnight, launch
2. tea, ocean garden, plants, birds
3. tug-of-war, egg-and-spoon
4. card room, ladies, allowed
5. captain, join, dinner, table, honor
6. seasick, spoonfuls, medicine
7. wait, gala ball, grand ballroom
8. •-- •• ••• ••••/-•-- --- ••-/
•-- • •-• •/•••• • •-• •/
•• •••- •/-••• • • -•/
• -••- •-- -•• --- ••- •• -• --•/
•-•- -•• ••• •/••• •- --.

9. •• /-- •• ••• •••/-•-- --- ••-/
•- -•-• •-•.

57

## Treasures from the Trunk, page 32

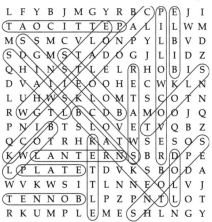

L F Y B J M G Y R B C P E J I
T A O C I T T E P A L I L W M
M S S M C V L O N P Y L B V D
S D G M S T A D O G J L I D Z
Q H I N S T L E L R H O B I S
D V A I I O O H E C W K L N
L U H W S K L O M T S C O T N
R W G T L B C B A M O O J Q
P N I B T S L O V E T V Q B Z
Q C O T R H K A T W S E S O S
K W L A N T E R N S B R D P E
L P L A T E T D V K S B O D A
W V K W S I T L N N E O L V J
T E N N O B L P Z P N T L O T
R K U M P L E M E S H L N G Y

## States in a Circle, page 33

Oregon, Washington, Idaho

## Christmas Surprise, page 34

| K | E | E | P | | H | I | D | D | E | N |
| | | | | U | N | T | I | L | | |
| C | H | R | I | S | T | M | A | S | | D | A | Y |

## Riddle Cross-Out, page 35

Milk when it turns sour

## Boarding House Hunt, page 36

1. Six—five beds and one sofa
2. Kitchen
3. Living room sofa
4. Dining room
5. Living room
6. Three in the bathroom and three in the kitchen
7. Under the bed
8. Two—one in the attic and one next to the bed in the living room
9. On the man playing checkers and on the table in the living room
10. Two hand mirrors on two dressers (upstairs bedroom and living room bedroom); in the bathroom; above the dresser in the living room bedroom
11. By the back door
12. On the dresser in the upstairs bedroom
13. Attic
14. Under the kitchen sink
15. The boy playing checkers in the dining room is sitting on it.

## To Freedom!, page 38

*Penny >*

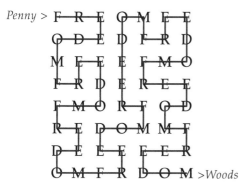

*>Woods*

## Sewing Shop Scramble, page 39

| | | | |
|---|---|---|---|
| buttons | ribbons | thread | scissors |
| fabric | yarn | lace | needle |

Love keeps a family together.

## Fandango Fun, page 42

Final answer: To celebrate a safe return.

## Ship-Speak Scramble, page 44

## Secrets Solved, page 40

## Animal Affections, page 45

| | |
|---|---|
| Fox Tail | Bear Blanket |
| Raven | Sparrow |
| Two Hawks | Swan Circling |
| Brown Deer | To Soar Like an Eagle |
| Little Fawn | |

# Gifts of Giving, page 46

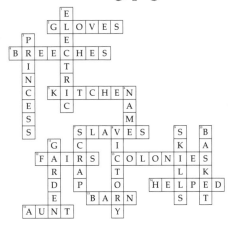

# Stories to Celebrate, page 50

1. Felicity finds her horse, Penny.
2. Josefina's father marries Tía Dolores.
3. Molly's father returns home from the war.
4. Kaya is reunited with Speaking Rain.
5. Kit's letter is published in the newspaper.
6. Samantha's uncle adopts Nellie and her sisters.
7. Addy's family is together again in Philadelphia.
8. Kirsten's family gets their very own house.
9. Hold on to your dreams.